O La_

Lanoo: a student, or seeker after truth.

- Do you want to know more about *O Lanoo!*?
- Do you have questions for Harvey Tordoff?
- Would you like to join an email discussion group with other readers of *O Lanoo!* and Harvey Tordoff ?
- Would you like to know more about Nina O'Connell, who created the illustrations for *O Lanoo!*?
- Would you like to buy postcards with some of the illustrations of *O Lanoo!*?

then we invite you to visit

www.olanoo.com

O Lanoo!

The Secret Doctrine Unveiled

Harvey Tordoff

Illustrated by
Nina O'Connell

FINDHORN
Press

© Harvey Tordoff 1999

First published in 1999

ISBN 1 899171 62 2

British Library Cataloguing-in-Publication Data.
A catalogue record for this book is available
from the British Library.

Layout by Pam Bochel
Illustrations (including front cover) by Nina O'Connell
Cover design by Thierry Bogliolo

Printed and bound by WSOY, Finland

Published by

Findhorn Press

The Park, Findhorn,   P. O. Box 13939
Forres IV36 3TY   Tallahassee
Scotland, UK   Florida 32317-3939, USA
Tel 01309 690582   Tel (850) 893 2920
Fax 01309 690036   Fax (850) 893 3442
e-mail info@findhornpress.com
http://www.findhornpress.com

INTRODUCTION

From the roof of The Potala, the palace of the exiled Dalai Lama, I looked down on the city of Lhasa. I had been ill in Kathmandu, and needed a wheelchair to get from Lhasa airport to the waiting bus, and now, in the thin air 12,000 feet above sea level, I had to stop for a rest every few steps. It felt like the end of a pilgrimage, and in fact The Potala is the ultimate pilgrimage for thousands of Buddhists from all over Tibet. But for me the pilgrimage did not begin at Lhasa airport, or even in Nepal, but thirty years earlier in a small terrace house in the North of England.

As a teenager I read indiscriminately — from James Bond and The Saint, Science Fiction and Fantasy, to books on religion and philosophy. I read about many exotic lands, some of which I would visit in later life, but Tibet was special. Tibet's ethos was spiritual, and the land was so ancient that legends told of caverns with relics of earlier civilisations. When I walked through the monasteries and temples, they were so familiar that I could not tell whether it was just that I had read about them or whether I had been there in a previous life. Although I have no specific memories, reincarnation was something I came to accept at an early age.

I trained to be an accountant, got married, and for many years had very little time for reading, but all through the business world my beliefs stayed with me. As the books I had read as a teenager (*Egyptian Book of the Dead, Tibetan Book of the Dead* etc.) faded from my memory, one book continued to influence my life. It was *The Secret Doctrine*, by Madame Blavatsky. I had only read the abridged version, and there was a lot in it I could not understand, but it seemed to contain a complete philosophy that added substance to my simple law of probability.

I became the Financial Director of a computer company which floated on the London Stock Exchange. It was not a life designed for inner contemplation, but although I did not always live up to my own ideals I was able to retain a certain level of integrity. Our corporate 'mission' was "to make as much money as we can today, providing that doesn't stop us making even more money tomorrow", which seemed compatible with my own 'mission statement': "Live in the moment, but don't forget that within the moment is the essence of the moment to come."

The time came when I was able to walk away from the rat race. With my wife and son I came to live in an isolated house in the English Lake District where I joined two local Buddhist groups. It was almost like living on a retreat, and for the first few years I worked in the woods, digging ditches, clearing fallen trees, and letting the accumulated dross of the business world slip away. I knew that I wanted to write, to put something back into a community that I had so far only taken from. Whilst I had inflated my ego by making business deals all over the world, my wife had practiced as a counselor and worked as a volunteer at a crisis centre. In real terms my life had seemed quite shallow. My wife set me on the path by buying me another copy of *The Secret Doctrine*.

I read it again, now with more maturity. I bought the original version, unabridged, and read that. It had everything in it, and yet it was so difficult to read. Surely it deserved to be read more widely. Eventually it dawned on me that this was a task that I was equipped to tackle. I had the patience of an auditor sifting through masses of information, and I had spent years distilling complex technical proposals into business reports for laymen. I could re-write the basic story of *The Secret Doctrine*.

Madame Helena Petrovna Blavatsky was born in southern Russia in 1831. She was a gifted child — a natural linguist, pianist, artist, and rider of half-broken horses — with psychic ability. She was also rebellious, and at eighteen married the middle-aged Nickifor Blavatsky simply because her governess taunted her that she would never marry anyone. The marriage was never consummated and Helena left her husband to travel, in Eastern Europe, Egypt, Greece, and in 1851 in London she made her first 'contact' with the Tibetan master who was to guide her later writings. During the next twenty years she travelled widely, in the United States, Japan, India, Nepal and Tibet, undergoing occult training and cleansing herself for a life of service.

In 1875 The Theosophical Society was founded in New York, with H.S. Olcott, an American lawyer, as President, and H.P.B. (as she became known) as Recording Secretary. The word 'Theosophy' means 'Divine Wisdom', and the aim of the society was to "collect and diffuse a knowledge of the laws which govern the Universe." There followed several books, papers and journals, and in 1888 *The Secret Doctrine* was published. H.P.B. said of this book: "These truths are in no sense put forward as a revelation, for what is contained in this work is to be found in thousands of volumes embodying the great Asiatic and early European religions, hidden under glyph and symbol. What is now attempted is to gather the oldest of the tenets together and to make of them one harmonious and unbroken whole. The aim is to show that Nature is not a fortuitous concurrence of atoms, and to assign to Man his rightful place in the scheme of the Universe."

H.P.B. died in 1891, but *The Secret Doctrine* is still regarded as the core teaching of The Theosophical Society. Now as then, however, the knowledge is largely inaccessible to those outside the Society, for the language and construction of the book are complex to the point of obfuscation. In the nineteenth century elitism was not uncommon, but as barriers are broken down at the end of the twentieth century, philosophical elitism seems totally inappropriate.

The Secret Doctrine begins: "An Archaic Manuscript — a collection of palm leaves made impermeable to water, fire, and air — is before the writer's eye." This manuscript is the Book of Dzyan, and H.P.B. translates a few hundred words, which by themselves reveal very little. She then writes fifteen hundred pages of explanation, interpretation, extrapolation and asides, and the story of Dzyan is all but lost. I have retold the *Book of Dzyan*, using H.P.B.'s explanations but ignoring all the side issues. I have tried to be faithful to the rich, poetical language of Dzyan, but avoided words that would be unfamiliar to the average reader. The result is a 10,000 word epic 'poem' which tells the story of the creation of the Universe and the evolution of Man.

Dzyan is written as if by a teacher for a student. The old Sanskrit word for student is 'Lanoo', and Dzyan addresses the student within the teachings: "It is they who are thou, me, him, Oh Lanoo. They who watch over thee." I have retained this word, and this format, and address the reader as 'Lanoo'. There was only one possible title: *O Lanoo!*

I have also tried to retain the style of writing, which reflects the content. If we are to make sense of our lives we need to learn to recognise patterns. We need to see the future we set in motion for ourselves by our actions and thoughts. We need to see the essence of tomorrow that is present today, and so the essence of the stanza to come is contained in the preceding stanza. As the veils are pulled aside there is a glimpse of what is still to come. Although this results in a certain amount of repetition it gives me the opportunity to say things in more than one way.

The first half of the book deals with the creation of the Universe. The language is different, but most of the ideas will be familiar. Western religions, for the most part, stop at a single creation, but here the 'Big Bang' which gave rise to our present Universe is presented merely as one in a series of big bangs. The Hindus describe it as part of the pattern of the breathing out and the breathing in of Brahma. If H.P.B. is correct, most modern religions have their own different versions of the creation but they are all based on the information inherited by our current 'Age'. The several creations and the appearance on Earth of Man were remembered by the Lemurians, and passed on to the Atlanteans, who left us incomplete records (including the *Book of Dzyan*). It is these accounts, enhanced and enriched, twisted and distorted, that were handed down through the generations to become the sacred words of God engraved in stone in the religions of today.

The second half of the book is concerned with the evolution of Man, and this contains concepts which might be more controversial. The beings of the first 'Race' were more like gods than men, and being non-physical they could 'occupy' Earth before the planet stabilised. This Race of Gods gave way to Races more and more corporeal, eventually coming together with the physical forms produced by natural evolution. The 'Spirit' of 'God' gradually fragmented and the individual sparks experienced life in the bodies of creatures on Earth. Each one of us has this 'spark' of God within (in fact, is a spark of God) and has experienced countless lives in this Age, in the last Age (of Atlantis) and the Age before that (Lemuria). In the Ages before Lemuria the sparks had not really separated, but we all shared that experience, and in the Ages to come we will eventually return to a similar state of union. We journey through Matter, from Spirit of innocence to Spirit of wisdom. We should never lose sight of the fact that we are all part of the same whole, and to harm others is to harm ourselves.

I had almost completed *O Lanoo!* when I visited Tibet. I arrived without baggage of any kind, physical or emotional, and my pride and ego were left behind when I crawled into the wheelchair. It was the perfect preparation for what was to be a profound spiritual experience. When I came home I made the final revisions, and I would like to think that some essence of Tibet is embodied in this book.

Many people today recognise that they are on a spiritual journey of some kind, and there are many books to help. The vast majority, however, are aimed at providing techniques and guidance which will enhance personal development or well being. *O Lanoo!* does not seek to do this, or to replace such books, but to provide a bigger picture of the landscape through which the spiritual journey takes place. I remember a Buddhist monk once saying that the world doesn't need anything else; it has sufficient resources and food for all; what the world needs is less ignorance so that we can make better and fairer use of what we have. Perhaps the world doesn't need one more book; but if after reading *O Lanoo!* more people start to treat other individuals, other societies and other life forms (or as the Buddhists would say, all sentient beings) with more respect, then the world will be a more harmonious place. That is what I want this book to achieve.

Harvey Tordoff
Cumbria
1 December 1998

PREFACE

"An Archaic Manuscript – a collection of palm leaves – is before the writer's eye." Thus begins *The Secret Doctrine* of Madame Helena Petrovna Blavatsky, the book which provided the inspiration for O Lanoo!

The Archaic Manuscript is the *Book of Dzyan*. The word "Dzyan", Blavatsky suggests, denotes a second, inner birth, in which one reforms one's self by meditation and knowledge. The seven stanzas of Cosmogenesis tell of the creation and evolution of the Universe, and the twelve stanzas of Anthropogenesis tell the story of Humankind*. *The Secret Doctrine* expands the few pages of Dzyan into a forbidding tome of fifteen hundred pages, in which Blavatsky distills the work of many teachers from many cultures to form the basic philosophy of Theosophy. It is one of the most intriguing books of the nineteenth century.

The Secret Doctrine has, however, overshadowed the *Book of Dzyan*, and *O Lanoo!* seeks to redress the balance. In retelling the story hidden in those ancient stanzas the author has drawn on the explanations given by Blavatsky whilst ignoring the many secondary themes she develops at length. The result is a rich and powerful book which offers a new level of understanding of the spiritual purpose of life on earth. Without favouring any religion or creed it describes the terrain over which the individual's spiritual path unfolds. The aim of the book is to enable the reader to feel more connected to other people, other life forms, and the planet as a whole, thus bringing the world one small step closer to the harmony which is our ultimate destiny.

* *In her translation of the Book of Dzyan, and throughout The Secret Doctrine, Blavatsky uses the word 'Man' to denote Humankind. Without intending any gender favouritism, and in the absence of a single syllable alternative, Harvey Tordoff has used 'Man' in like manner.*

CONTENTS

Part One

THE SEVEN CREATIONS

Part Two

THE JOURNEY OF THE PILGRIM SOUL

Man and the Universe
Came together in the ancient sound of OM:
The perfect circle of infinity,
The eternal Ohhhhhh of the Universe
And Mmmmmmm,
The vibration of Man;

M, the hieroglyph of Water,
The symbol for the feminine aspect of Nature,
The root of Mare, the Sea,
And Mary, Mother of Jesus,

And Maya, illusion, Mother of Buddha,
And all drawn from the Motion of the Moon
From whence sprang all Life.

Part One

THE SEVEN CREATIONS

In the beginning, which is also the end,
there was the long Night of Rest

STANZA I: Before Creation

1. In the beginning,
   Which is also the end,
   There was the long Night of Rest;
   A Night devoid of all but Space,
   The eternal Parent;
   A Night which to you,
   O Lanoo,
   Would be eternity,
   Or rather, seven eternities,
   For as there are seven Great Ages
   Of the Day,
   So also are there seven Great Ages
   Of the Night.

   But Space is not a limitless void;
   She contains all the latent Matter
   And essence
   Of Creation.

2. Time did not exist,
   For what is Time
   Without a state of consciousness?

   The illusion of Time
   Was waiting to be born
   With your perception of changing Matter.

3. The Universal Force
   Which you would call God
   Was not,
   For there was no Life
   In which to manifest.

4. The seven paths leading to Nirvana
    Did not exist

    There was no-one to seek
    The wisdom
    And knowledge
    Which provide release
    From the world of ignorance
    You now inhabit,
    O Lanoo,
    For there was no suffering,
    And no-one to be deceived
    By illusion.

5. The Spirit and the substance
    Of the manifested Universe
    Of the previous Round
    Were as one
    In the Darkness;
    The Father
    And the Mother
    And the Son
    Were once more One,
    The eternal matrix
    In which at the end of the Night
    The source of Light
    Would once again appear.

    There was no polarity of light and dark,
    Or male and female;
    There was not as yet
    The differentiation
    Between Spirit and Matter
    Which would give rise
    To the Creation of the finite Universe
    Of this great cycle of being.

6. The seven Creative Spirits,
   Each of whom was to bring about
   One of the seven Great Ages,
   Had ceased to be.

   The seven noble truths
   Were waiting to be revealed,
   One by one,
   Age by age.

   The Universe you now know,
   O Lanoo,
   Just one in a chain of evolving universes,
   Was yet to be created
   From the absolute perfection
   Attained at the close
   Of the last great cycle.

   All was naught.

7. In all sentient Life
   The desire to exist had ceased;
   In every atom
   The impulse to be had ceased;
   And all that had been
   And all that was
   And all that was to be
   Rested in the Absolute Oneness
   Of eternal Space,
   And it was from this state of rest,
   O Lanoo,
   That Creation began.

For if your God's creation
Was accomplished in six ages
Would He then
Like some Mortal
Be in need of rest?
Nay, the day of rest
Preceded the flash of Light
In the Darkness.

8. That which was to become Life
Pulsated unconsciously
Within the essence of the Universal Force
Which, alone and dormant,
Omnipresent and abstract,
Stretched boundless,
Causeless,
Infinite.

9. But where,
O Lanoo,
Was the purified Soul of Man
When the Soul of the Universe
Was not conscious;
When the great cycle of being
Of this Universe
Had not been conceived?

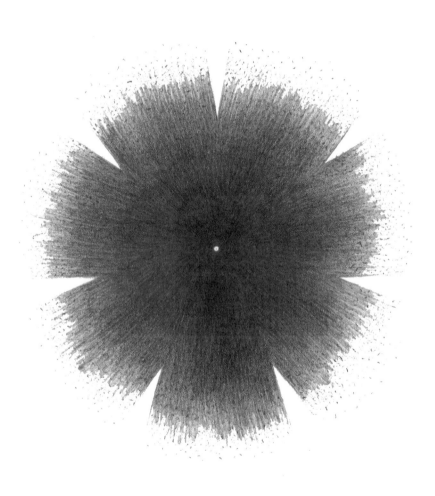

Your God, O Lanoo, had not yet said:
"Let there be Light"

STANZA II: THE ESSENCE OF THE CREATION
TO COME

1. And where,
    O Lanoo,
    Were the seven Creative Spirits,
    Who would emerge
    From the long Night of Rest
    And create the finite Universe
    From the seven Cosmic Elements?

    In the unknowable Darkness
    Of absolute perfection
    The purified Soul of Man
    Rested with your Creators
    In the bliss
    Of non-being
    As the elements
    Of hydrogen
    And oxygen
    Rest in water.

2. And where was silence?
    Where were the ears to sense it?
    Nay, there was neither silence
    Nor sound;
    Naught, save unconscious,
    Ceaseless,
    Eternal motion.

    It was the eternal
    Momentary pause
    In the breathing of Brahma,
    Following the inhalation
    Which had ended the last great cycle,
    And before the exhalation
    Which was to be your expanding Universe.

3. The moment had not come:
    The Ray of Light in the Darkness
    Had not yet flashed into the essence of Matter;
    Matter and energy had not yet produced
    The heat and moisture of Life.

4. Still latent was the Ether
    Which was to receive the spark
    Of immaculate conception,
    Thence to give rise
    To the virgin birth
    Of the finite Universe.

    The three higher Elements
    Had not yet combined
    With Fire, Air, Water and Earth,
    The four lower Elements
    That would mark the boundaries
    Of your world of illusion,
    O Lanoo.

5. The seven Creative Spirits
    Were not yet born
    From the web of Light.
    The Father-Mother of Creation;
    The eternal energy
    Of the Universal Soul;
    The fundamental Law
    Of Cause and Effect;
    All still rested in Darkness.

6. The Universe had yet to become
    A Divine Thought;
    The Universe,
    Son of God,
    Had yet to be conceived.

Your God,
O Lanoo,
Had not yet said:
"Let there be Light!"

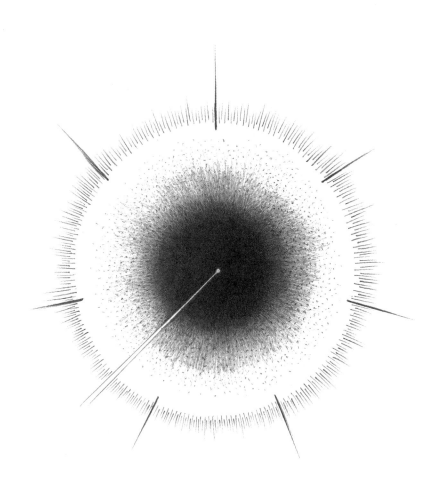

The last vibration of the long Night of Darkness
became the first vibration of the Day

STANZA III: The Re-awakening of the Universe

1. At the end
   Of the seventh eternity
   Of the Night of Brahma,
   The last vibration
   Of the long Night of Darkness
   Becomes the first vibration
   Of the Day.

   Within the infinite reaches of Space
   The Universal Matrix swells
   Like the bud of the lotus.

2. The vibration thrills through infinity,
   Touching the germ that dwells in the Darkness;
   Moving over the deep slumbering waters of
   Space,
   Mother of Life,
   Wherein rests
   Latent Spirit
   Containing latent Matter.

3. From within the Darkness
   One solitary Ray of Light
   Drops into the Ether
   And shoots through
   The virgin-egg of Space.

   Divine Thought
   Impregnates primordial Space,
   And the Mother gives birth
   To the non-eternal Universe.

4. Homogeneous Space
   Containing the essence
   Of all that is to be
   Becomes differentiated Space.

   The three Elements of Spirit
   Fall into the four Elements of Matter
   And the radiant essence
   Takes on seven aspects.

   The light, heat and moisture
   Generated by the motion
   Of the out-breath of Brahma
   Produce Matter,
   And every atom
   Vibrates with Life.

   Within a Universe
   Which will evolve
   Through seven Ages
   Life will evolve
   Through seven stages.

   The virgin-egg of Space
   Now filled with Light
   Curdles
   And the origins of Matter
   Contained in the essence of Spirit
   Spread like milky whey
   Throughout the depths of Space.

5. The Absolute Oneness
    Of eternal Space remains;
    The pure knowledge
    Of all that is
    And was
    And is to be
    Remains;
    The Ray of Light remains;
    The origins of Matter remain;
    Yet all are manifestations
    Of the Universal Force
    Which had rested
    In the long Night of Darkness.

6. And even as the essence of Light
    Had rested in the Absolute Darkness,
    So now darkness is transformed into Light,
    And the essence of Darkness rests
    In an ocean of radiant Light.

    The essence of Fire
    And heat
    And motion,
    The essence of Life itself,
    Is in every atom,
    Every drop
    Of the ocean of immortality.

    Darkness vanishes
    And is no more:
    Thus is born Lucifer,
    Light,
    The first Son of God,
    The luminous Son of the Morning
    Of the first Great Age
    Of the new cycle.

7.   Behold, O Lanoo!
     Glorious bright Space,
     Son of dark Space,
     The radiant child
     Of the Divine Ray,
     Who emerges from the depths
     Of the great dark waters of Space!

     This is not a Creation;
     This is not a son born of parents;
     This is a Universe,
     A re-creation,
     A transformation
     Of that which went before.

     This Son is the blazing Dragon of Wisdom
     In which dwell the seven Spirits of Creation,
     And the hosts
     And multitudes of Spirits
     To follow.

     The four aspects of Matter
     Take on the three aspects of Spirit
     And the union
     Produces the differentiated Universe,
     Which will be home to Man.

And as with the Universe
So with the solar system;
On this, your Earth,
Your Sun moves from East to West,
Obscuring the reality above
And illuminating your world of illusion
Where you see
Many differentiated aspects
And transformations
Which you do not recognise
As manifestations of the Divine Essence,
Of the One Universal Element,
Which is unborn,
Undying,
Infinite.

8. Now all that had been
And all that was
And all that was to be
Rested in the Light,
The white brilliant Light.

But where now is the germ of all new Life,
Where now is Darkness?
And where is the Spirit of the flame
That burns in your lamp,
O Lanoo?
Where is the Flame of your Spirit?

How can you say
That the Light in you
Is not the same Light
That shines in all sentient beings,
Transformed from the Darkness
At the beginning of Time?
From where else
Would come your Spirit?

The germ of all new Life
Is That which you would call God,
And God is Light,
Son of Darkness.

9. The first light was a cold flame,
For heat could not exist
Before the differentiation of Matter.

But flame is Fire
And as the Universe materialises
Fire produces heat
Which yields Water,
The Water of Life
In the great chaos of Creation.

The Fire and Water were not yet
The Fire and Water
Of the world of Matter,
For this was not yet a physical Universe;
But before Fire and Water
Could exist
There had to be
The essence
Of Fire
And Water.

10. And as these primordial Elements
Swirled and coalesced
Some parts became more dense,
Giving the Universe a spectrum
From shimmering Spirit
To leaden Matter,
And yet the whole remained
An interconnected web
Of universal Cause and Effect.

11. This web,
    This Universe,
    Expands and contracts
    As energy flows;
    Expanding through Spirit,
    Contracting through Matter.

    This rhythmic pulsing
    Of the Universe
    Can be seen in all living things,
    For there is vibration
    In every atom.

    Then the Sons of Creation,
    The seven Cosmic Elements,
    Dissociate and scatter,
    Expanding and contracting
    In their own right,
    Not to be re-joined
    As the One Universal Element
    Until the end
    Of the Great Day
    Of Brahma.

12. The Cosmic Elements
    Divide into the common elements
    As cosmic electricity
    Infuses the atoms
    With energy,
    Naturally,
    Through the Law
    Of Cause and Effect,
    And a Universe
    Of countless worlds
    Of Matter
    Is created.

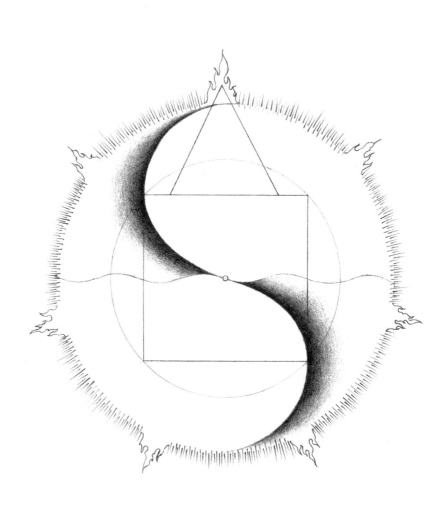

And with the building blocks of the Cosmic Elements. . . .
Matter was created

STANZA IV: CREATION OF THE GODS

1. Listen, O Lanoo!
   Listen to those from whom you can learn:
   The Sons of Fire,
   Radiating energy of pure Spirit;
   First beings to evolve from primordial Fire;
   Fashioners of the Inner Being.

   Listen, son of Earth,
   Learn that no manifestation,
   Not even Time,
   Can be understood
   Except as part of a larger whole.

   It is not that what you see
   And feel
   And touch
   And hear
   Does not exist;
   But that which you see
   Or feel
   Or touch
   Or hear
   Is but the tip of an iceberg:
   One aspect revealed;
   Six aspects concealed.

   And all seven aspects
   Are the manifestation
   Of the Divine Essence;

This is your illusion,
O Lanoo,
For you believe
That you can isolate,
Examine,
Analyse,
One aspect
Of each manifestation
On your material world
And in so doing
You believe you see
And understand the whole.

2.   Listen, O Lanoo!
     Listen and learn;
     Learn what we,
     Descended from the primordial seven Creative Spirits,
     Who are born from the primordial Flame of Spirit,
     Have learnt from our fathers.

3.   From the radiance of Light
     Of the one spark
     Emanating from within the Darkness
     Of that eternal Night
     There emerged the re-awakened energies of Creation.

Within the abstract circle of Space,
Governed by the mystic pi,
The energies and forces
Divide and sub-divide
Into the sacred numbers
That provide the key
To the structure of the Universe,
And within that Universe
To the essences and energies,
And the elements and builders
Of Divine Man,
The heavenly Zodiac,
And the physical four-square world of Matter.

4. First to appear
    In the Darkness
    Which preceded Creation
    Was Light;
    Then followed Sound.

    Sounds
    And words
    And names
    Possess their own inherent power,
    For within Thought
    Lies the essence of Matter,
    And sounds
    Give expression to Thought.

And the seven Creative Spirits
With their different voices and names
Contain the blueprints
For the seven races of Man;
And although each Being
Within each race
Is unique,
Each Being
Is a materialised
As yet imperfect expression
Of the Divine Spark.

And evolution began with the egg,
The empty circle of abstract Space,
Without meaning,
In which appeared
A central point,
Like the germ of the lotus
Within its seed;
The point of potentiality
Transforms into the line
Dividing the circle
Into noumena and phenomena,
Heaven and Earth,
Spirit and Matter;
Then comes the further division
Of phenomena
Into the Tau
Of creative and passive energy,
Of male and female,
Which becomes the mundane cross
Of Man.

On seven levels
This progression was repeated;
The One becomes two
Becomes three
Becomes four
Then five and six and seven,
And with the building blocks
Of the Cosmic Elements
And the shapes of simple compounds
Matter was created.

5. Within the eternal motion of Space,
Within the Darkness,
Within the unborn,
Undying,
Unknowable,
Is the Cause,
The point;
Not yet the Creator
But the Cause of the Creator.

The point in the boundless circle,
The flash of Light
In the infinite Darkness,
Is the essence of Creation;
The Divine Thought
Of that indefinable force.

And with the Sound
That followed the flash of Light,
The Thought
Becomes the Word.
And with that Word
The seven Creative Spirits
Of the seven Cosmic Elements
Proclaim the birth
Of the finite Universe.

And the first condensation of Matter
Took place around a central nucleus,
Which fragmented into an expanding Universe
Of countless suns and planets,
Including your Sun,
O Lanoo,
And the planets of your Sun.

Thus did the Sons of Light,
The suns of the Universe,
Emerge from the primeval chaos
And clothe themselves in Matter.

6. And Creation cascades
Through seven levels of Spirit
Falling ever further
From the Divine Essence.

From the Word
And the Voice
And the Spirit
Of the seven Creative Forces
Come the seven Guardians of the Sky,
The Recorders of all Life;
For every act
And every thought
That ever was
And is
And will be
Impresses itself on the Ether
To become a part
Of the continuing miracle of Creation.

*Divine Thought . . . passes like lightning through the stellar mists
and in each mote of cosmic dust sets in motion the laws of evolution*

STANZA V: THE CREATION OF THE GALAXIES

1. The seven Creative Spirits,
    First seven breaths
    Of the Dragon of Wisdom,
    Produce the cosmic dust
    That forms the building blocks of Matter.

    Each mote of dust,
    Each atom,
    Contains the dormant Divine Spark,
    Which is awakened
    Through self-experience
    In Matter
    And in Spirit.

2. Spurred by the seven Creative Spirits
    Divine Thought,
    Now manifesting as dynamic creative energy,
    Passes like lightning
    Through the stellar mists
    And in each mote of cosmic dust
    Sets in motion
    The laws of evolution.

    The Divine Ray
    Passes through Spirit
    And into Soul,
    And through Soul
    And into Matter,
    The three strides of the original Fall
    Which would become confused
    With the Fall of Man.

The two lower planes
Of consciousness and being,
The Terrestrial and the Astral,
Support the five upper planes,
And upon these seven planes of existence
Would unfold the evolution of the galaxies,
And the seven Ages of Man
On his seven continents
On his seven spheres.

Divine Thought becomes the Word;
The Word is spoken
And atoms
Are joined together in Matter.

3.   Through this dynamic, creative energy
The atoms settle
In their natural order,
Spinning off the molecules
Of the mineral kingdom
Which float and sparkle
In gaseous clouds,
Gyrating in universal motion
On planes that connect the triangles
Of Matter and Spirit,
Form and no-form.

4.   In all entities Evolution spirals
Around the central core of Karma
Through six planes to the Crown,
In the atom and in the planet,
In the galaxy and in Man,
Watched over by Angelic Beings
Throughout the seven eternities.

The formless first world
Of Divine Thought
Becomes the shadowy second world
Of primal form;
This is the first world of illusion,
O Lanoo,
For how can you see
Beyond the shadows?

But even though you see
Many lights in the sky,
And the many lights of Human Souls,
Perhaps you can sense
That there is
But one flame.

5. The five higher planes of consciousness
    Evolve one from the other,
    Out of the dynamic creative energy.

    At each of the cardinal points
    Of the mystic tabernacle
    Is a cosmic force
    That sweeps in like a wind
    From North and South,
    From East and West,
    Carrying the secrets
    Of the Universe
    For those whose minds are open.

And within each cosmic force
Is a host of minor forces,
The energies which rebuild the finite Universe
After each long night of Brahma;
Those which create the stars and planets;
And those which created your planetary chain
And the ancestors of Man,
For the destinies of Man and Nature
Are governed by these swirling energies.

6.   The Guardians of the Sky,
     The Recorders of Karma,
     Separate the finite from the infinite,
     The upper triangle of the plane of Spirit
     From the four-square world of Matter.

     They draw a karmic circle
     Around the personal ego,
     An impassable barrier
     For those who are not yet freed
     From the ties of ignorance;
     For those who are not yet ready
     To re-merge with the Divine Essence.

     And so it will remain
     Until the end of the Great Day,
     And the next long Night is upon us.

The globe of Fire became a globe of Fire and Air,
which became a globe of Fire, Air and Water,
which became the Earth you now inhabit, O Lanoo

STANZA VI: THE CREATION OF EARTH

1. The Word of God
   Penetrated the egg of Space
   And Divine Thought made manifest was born.

   The all-pervading wisdom
   Of the Father
   And the all-encompassing compassion
   Of the Mother
   Came together in a new-born Son,
   The seven-aspected non-eternal Universe.

2. From the constant motion
   Around the active and passive principles
   Of Light and Darkness
   Came the energies and atoms
   Of the seven planes of existence
   Of the finite universe.

   This is how evolution progresses;
   Not through brute matter,
   Blind force,
   Senseless motion,
   But sentient life
   In intelligent law
   Guided from above.

3. The seven Great Elements
   Found throughout the Universe,
   Evolving from the one element
   Of Divine Spirit
   Are revealed one by one.

In two billion years,
O Lanoo,
Your four Ages
Have given you Fire
And Air
And Water
And Earth,
The aspects you know as
Energy, gases, liquids and solids.

Now, before the dawning
Of the fifth Age,
The essence of Ether,
The fifth Element,
Can be sensed by those
Who are ready;
Ether, whose existence is hinted at
By those spectacular displays
Above the Earth's poles.

The common elements
Familiar to your scientists
Are of course peculiar to your system,
For the seven Great Elements
Appear in many forms on other worlds.

And as each of the seven Elements is revealed
The planet evolves to the next stage:
The globe of Fire
Became a globe of Fire and Air,
Which became a globe
Of Fire, Air and Water,
Which became the Earth
You now inhabit,
O Lanoo,
For this is the fourth
In a chain of seven globes.

4. And so Divine Thought made manifest,
   This Virgin Son,
   Sparks through the cosmic dust
   Creating balls of Fire,
   Setting them in motion,
   Infusing them with Life.

   For with Fire and motion
   The condition of the Elements is changed
   And worlds are formed
   According to the worlds
   That have gone before,
   Before the long Night of Rest,
   Acting out the Law of Cause and Effect
   Set in motion
   In the last Great Day.

   And as Spirit descends into differentiation,
   Into the polarity of positive and negative energy,
   The potential for conflict arises.
   The wonderful opportunities offered
   By sensory experience
   And disharmony
   Are maximised on the physical plane
   Which dominates this part
   Of the Fourth Great Age.

STANZA VI (Aside)

This is the story of the Cosmos:
Not so much the story of Creation
As the story of Evolution,
For in truth
Nothing is created.

The Absolute Oneness
Of the long Night of Rest
Transforms,
Evolves,
Manifests,
On the different planes
Of the long Day of Brahma.

But as above, so below,
And for those who can see
Beyond the words,
The story of the Cosmos
Is also the story
Of the solar system,
And Earth,
And Man.

That which evolves
Can only evolve
From the essence
Of that which is to evolve;
The deed evolves
From the essence of the deed,
From the thought.

The Earth evolved
From the essence of the Earth,
Which in the cosmic fiery dust
Was without substance or form.

As Spirit descended into Matter
The essence of Earth,
The ethereal planet,
Hardened and adopted the shape
Of the planet you now know
As Mother Earth.

Thus evolution progresses
Through a series of stages or globes,
O Lanoo,
Each containing the essence
Of the globe to follow.

This dense world of Matter
Is not the ultimate achievement of evolution,
But merely one link
In a chain
Which will contain more globes
Ascending now towards Spirit.

This is the Universal pattern:
Seven Globes;
Seven Rounds;
Seven Ages,
In which Spirit
Passes through seven states of being.

Then the triple strands of evolution,
Spirit, intellect and form,
Come together in Man,
From whence the Spirit,
Now with the self-knowledge
And wisdom
Of experience,
Can move to the next cycle
On the path
To the Absolute Oneness
Of the Divine Essence.

It is as though the moisture
In some vast ocean
Had been burnt up by a fiery sun,
Evaporated to form clouds in the air,
Fallen as drops of rain on the ground,
Collected in pools
And flowed as streams
And rivers,
Over rocks and earth
To form again one vast ocean;
The same drops
Of the same moisture
Within the same ocean,
Yet changed by the passage
Through and over those alien elements.

Before you ask why,
O Lanoo,
Ask yourself this:
Can Man
On this fourth globe,
This world of illusion,
Hope to comprehend the Infinite?
If you were so small
That you could see the atoms
Of your Mother's body,
Wheeling like vast solar systems,
Could you imagine
Her true nature?
At night when you look at the stars
In The Milky Way,
Can you imagine
What you are really looking at?
Could you comprehend if you were told?

It is enough
That you know
That you are a Pilgrim-Soul,
On a journey shared by all Beings,
Through the cycle of Humanity,
Through the cycle of Earth,
Through the cycle of the Cosmos,
As you move ever closer
To the Eternal Source.

STANZA VI (continued)

5.   In each of the seven Great Ages
     Of Planet Earth
     There are seven Races of Man.

     In the first three Races
     Man, like Earth,
     Was not yet solid;
     In this,
     The fourth Great Age,
     The Spirit of Man
     Had to clothe itself
     In Matter;
     This was the Fall:
     Not the Fall of Man
     Into sin
     But the Fall of Spirit
     Into Matter.

     The Beings who developed
     In the first three Great Ages
     Had now to experience
     The world of Matter,
     And though there were those Creative Spirits
     Who accepted physical incarnation
     In these hardening bodies,
     One-third refused.

     This was the action
     Which would result in suffering,
     The lot of physical Beings on Earth,
     For the schism between the Gods of Creation
     Contained the essence of conflict,
     Now manifesting in Man
     On a plane where conflict
     Can be expressed in violence between individuals,
     And in war between nations.

6. It is the substance of the old,
    Containing the essence of the new,
    Which gives way to become
    The substance of the new.

    Thus after many aeons
    The ethereal globe
    Has been transformed
    Into this physical Earth,
    The fourth globe,
    And the ethereal Spirit of Man
    Has been imprisoned in Material Man,
    Living now
    On the fourth plane
    Wherein lies the essence
    Of the higher planes to come.
    And in the Cosmos
    Creation continues
    As spiritually-charged particles
    Move through space,
    Some disintegrating in destruction,
    Some coalescing,
    Creating stronger masses,
    Forming globes
    Which ultimately
    Will bear life.

    But the destiny of Man
    Is to attune
    The seven inner states of consciousness
    To those of the Universe;
    This you can only do,
    O Lanoo,
    By activating them,
    By living in them,
    And by understanding yourself
    And your relationship with the Cosmos.

7. This is the fourth globe
    Of Mother Earth;
    The first was homogeneous;
    The second aeriform and radiant;
    The third was curd-like,
    Nebulous;
    This fourth is atomic,
    Where particles of Matter
    Are differentiated;
    The fifth will be germinal,
    Fiery,
    The sixth vapoury
    And the seventh will be cold.

    And if you would know the age
    Of your small planet,
    O Lanoo,
    Then make your calculations,
    But not until you are ready
    Will this be meaningful;
    For as the student strives
    To become a master
    So he finds that as a master
    He is the student
    Of yet another master.

    It is only after harmonising
    The four lower levels
    Of consciousness,
    O Lanoo,
    That you can understand
    The physical globe of Earth;
    Only then will you move
    To the three higher levels
    That will lead you to Nirvana.

Spirit evolves through the seven Elements,
and within the Elements through the seven cycles of each kingdom

STANZA VII: THE CREATION OF MAN

1. Behold, O Lanoo!
   The beginning of sentient,
   Formless Life.

   The Universe,
   Son of God,
   Is born when the first Light
   Penetrates the Darkness;
   When the Wisdom of the Father
   Penetrates the Understanding of the Mother;
   Life on Earth is born
   When the Light of the Sun
   Strikes her Waters;
   Man, microcosmic Son of God,
   Is born when Spirit enters the body.

   First the One,
   The Divine Flame;
   Then the separation,
   From which comes the trinity
   Of Spirit, Soul and Mind,
   Which manifest
   In the substance of atoms,
   Making possible the formation of Man;
   For the Divine Flame exists
   Within Spirit, Soul and Mind,
   Which exist within Matter,
   Within the nature of Man.

   And awaiting their turn
   Are the spirits of the atoms;
   The thought forms,
   Elementals,
   And nature spirits;

Who will all follow
Their own long, long path
Of Evolution.

The shining seven,
The mind-born seven Creators,
Sons of the First Lord,
Contain the essences of the three higher
And the four lower principles;
But they are also you,
O Lanoo,
And me,
And him,
For in reality all are one.

And like guardian angels
It is they who watch over you,
And your Mother Earth.

2. Thus the Creators evolve
From the One Light,
Containing the essence
Of the seven Elements
From which is born sentient Life.

For there is Life in Fire,
And in Air,
And in Water,
Before ever Matter appears;
And there will be Life
When Matter is no more.

Your physical body,
O Lanoo,
Is one of many
Through which pass
Your higher principles,
And the physical world
Is just one stage
In your evolution;
Running through these countless existences
Is your life-ray,
Like a thread through many pearls.

3. In the Cosmos
   Darkness radiates Light
   And the One Ray of Light
   Manifests as the non-eternal Universe.

   In the microcosm which is Man
   This Ray of Light
   Forms the thread of re-birth
   On which hang the personalities
   With which you,
   O Lanoo,
   Identify all too readily,
   Claiming "This is me!"

4. Three spiritual flames burn brightly
   Above the four earthly wicks.
   But though the physical body
   Disintegrates with death
   And the energy of the three lower subtle bodies
   Is dissipated,
   Yet the three higher levels of Man,
   The divine Spirit and the spiritual Soul,
   Assimilating the achievements
   Of the human Mind,
   Go forward to the next rebirth.

The earth-bound bodies which to you,
O Lanoo,
Appear to sparkle with life
Are as the reflection of moonbeams
Shimmering on the ocean,
Their existence an illusion
Created by the Queen of the Night.

5.   The Universe evolves;
     The Earth evolves;
     Man evolves;
     Each progresses through seven stages,
     And the cycle of the evolution of Man
     Takes place within the cycle
     Of the evolution of Earth
     Within the evolution of the Universe.

     Spirit evolves through the seven Elements,
     And within the Elements
     Through the seven cycles of each kingdom.

     The One Ray of Light
     Evolves through the mineral kingdom
     To the plant kingdom,
     Where Spirit begins to differentiate
     Towards individual consciousness;
     Thence to the animal kingdom,
     Where in some species
     Spirit lives still in the collective,
     And then to the kingdom of Man;
     And beyond Man
     Pure Spirit moves on
     Until once more
     All that is and ever was
     Rests within the undifferentiated Presence
     You would call God.

Your ancestors claimed
That a stone becomes a plant,
Which becomes a beast,
Which becomes a man,
Which becomes a spirit,
Which becomes a god.
And whilst this over-simplifies
The nature of the Universe,
Yet it speaks of the interconnectedness
Of all Creation.

Therefore seek to understand the nature
Of these many cycles,
O Lanoo,
But seek not the "missing link",
For while Man and beast
Have much in common
Yet Man is not descended from the ape.

And there are wheels
Within wheels
Within wheels;
Cycles within cycles within cycles.
And each of your seven bodies
Is governed by an Element,
And each Element by a heavenly body,
And the cycle of Life on Earth
Is subject to the pull of the Moon.

And as Spirit descends into Matter
And Matter ascends towards Spirit
The substance which is Matter
Evolves its own characteristics,
Corresponding to the development
Of the seven senses of Man.

And like the worlds of the Universe
The atoms of Matter
Play host to multitudinous life forms;
Even the body of Man
Has its own evolution,
Building through five ages of seven years
And decaying over five ages of seven years;
And in each of those ages
The particles of Matter
Comprising the body of Man
Are born,
Evolve,
And die.

6. The Divine Ray
    Which is the essence of every Life
    And which in Man
    Manifests as Spirit
    Shines through the physical body
    More strongly,
    More radiant,
    With every incarnation;
    The promise of early morning sunlight
    Develops into noonday glory.

7. The Divine Essence
    Clothes itself in Spirit
    For the cycle which will end
    When all things
    Re-merge in divine unity,
    Just as the Spirit
    Clothes itself in Matter
    For the cycle which will end
    With the death of the body.

The Divine Essence,
Spirit and intellect,
Emotion and instinct,
The semi-corporeal and the physical;
These are the seven aspects of Man,
The holy trinity of the Higher Self
Rising from the four pillars
Of physical Life;
The microcosm of Man
Reflecting the macrocosm of the Universe.

Thus might you say,
O Lanoo,
That Man is made
In the image of God;
Or God is made
In the image of Man;
For God is Man in Heaven
And Man is God on Earth.

Part Two

THE JOURNEY OF THE PILGRIM SOUL

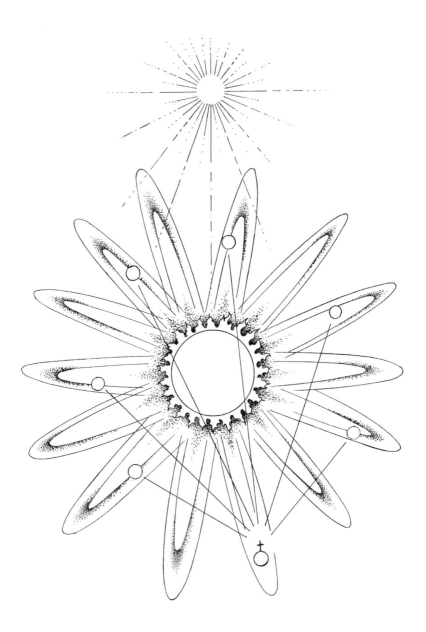

Spiritual Light radiates from the One Source, passing through the Spiritual Guardians, where it is diffused and coloured by the characterisation and planet of each Guardian as it falls to Earth

STANZA I: EARTH, HOME OF MAN

1. The Spiritual Guardian of this,
   The fourth globe in Earth's chain,
   Is one of seven wise servants
   Who drive their planets
   Like chariots
   Around the Sun.

   The Sun gives light
   And Life
   To Mother Earth
   As the spiritual Son,
   Divine Thought,
   Gives Life
   And Light
   To the Cosmos.

2. The Sun radiates
   His heat and light
   To all the planets,
   But Venus receives twice
   That which falls on Earth.

   Earth looks upon Venus
   As the precursor of the dawn
   And twilight;
   Venus, whose symbol is a globe
   Presiding over a cross;
   Spirituality presiding over generation.

   Venus, from whom Earth can learn,
   For the symbol of Earth
   Is a cross presiding over a globe;
   Matter dominating Spirit.

The Sun's rays fell sevenfold
On Mercury's Lords of Wisdom
And Earth looked to the Sun,
The Lord of the Shining Face,
For the light
To bring Life to Earth
As he had brought Life
To Mercury and Venus.

And though light comes direct from the Sun
Spiritual Light radiates from the One Source,
Passing through the Spiritual Guardians
Where it is diffused and coloured
By the characteristics
And planet
Of each Guardian
As it falls to Earth.

Thus it was that the First Race of Man
Was born under the Sun;
The Second under Jupiter;
The Third under Venus;
The Fourth under the Moon;
And this, the Fifth Race,
Under the influence of Mercury.

3.   The Lord of the Shining Face
Responded to Earth's cry,
And when she was ready
His heat and light were there
For the creation of Life.

But the spiritual Light
Which fell on Mercury
Granting immortality
Fell weakly on distant Earth,
Where wisdom remained too feeble
To dispel ignorance.

The cycle of Life on Earth
Was linked with the Moon,
Whose Spirit
And reflected light
Would move the creative waters
Of Earth and her creatures,
And Man,
Born to suffering
And living in illusion,
Was destined to be mortal.

4. The globe of Fire that was Earth
   Subsided at last
   And emerged from the three stages
   Of pre-physical evolution;
   Aeons of fiery, gaseous existence
   Which you would not recognize,
   O Lanoo,
   As capable of supporting Life.

In this Fourth Round
Of Mother Earth
Man would evolve
Through seven Races
And Earth would shudder
With the birth-pangs of each new Age
As land rose up
Or was swallowed by the sea
And a new dominant continent emerged.

And each time
Earth, like a serpent with a new skin,
Was ready for the next Race.

And through these seven Ages
Of seven Races
On the seven continents of Earth
Would journey
The Pilgrim-Soul of Man.

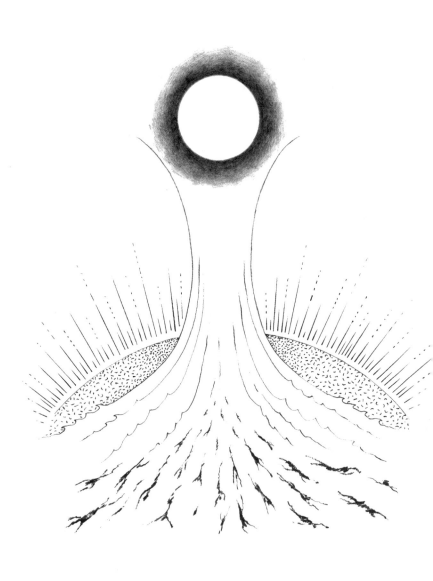

*The harsh Sun beat down and dried up the oceans,
and the fiery lower Spirits ended the evolutionary lines
of those soul-less creatures which could never be men*

STANZA II: NATURAL EVOLUTION

5. For 300 million years
    Earth whirled
    As she rushed through Space
    And eventually
    The elements coalesced.

    The forerunners of minerals appeared,
    And vegetation,
    And insect life,
    But in those early years,
    O Lanoo,
    Before she found a stable orbit,
    Earth was a violent place.

    Again and again she shook
    And tilted her axis,
    And from the oceans
    New life emerged
    Only to be destroyed
    With the next convulsion.

    Thus it came to pass
    That natural evolution produced
    The lower animal kingdoms
    And even a race
    Which could be said to resemble Man.

    But this first attempt at Man
    Created solely from Earth's elements
    Was soul-less
    And spirit-less;
    No more than an instinctual animal.

6. Thus did Mother Earth
    Make her animal-Man,
    Using only physical elements
    Derived from the minerals, vegetation and animals
    Of earlier evolution.

    And now the Spirits of the Sun
    And the Spirits of the Moon
    Came and looked
    At that which Earth had created.

7. Spirit descends gradually,
    Eventually accepting the constraints
    And distortions
    Of the awful prison of Matter,
    But when the Creative Spirits
    Saw the Earth-made man-creatures
    They recoiled in horror,
    For these bodies
    Were too gross for spiritual growth;
    Man could not be created
    By Nature unaided.

8. And so as Earth settled in her orbit
    The harsh Sun beat down
    And dried up the oceans,
    And the fiery lower Spirits
    Ended the evolutionary lines
    Of those soul-less creatures
    Which could never be men.

9. Mother Earth wept
    And the waters of her oceans
    Were lifted up towards the Moon
    From whence they came.

10. Bare land emerged from beneath the sea
    And the gross natural creatures were gone,
    And Earth was cleansed
    And bathed in solar light
    And spiritual Light.

    She was ready for the beginning
    Of new Life.

*Each of the seven Moon Gods
would govern one of Earth's seven continents*

STANZA III: THE CREATORS OF MAN

11. From the eternity
    Of the Night of Darkness
    The One Force
    Which is unknowable
    And unnamable
    Manifested
    As the non-eternal Universe.

    The energies released
    Were the creative forces
    Of the galaxies,
    And within the Solar System
    The birth of the life-giving Sun,
    And the Queen of the Night,
    And Earth herself,
    Released the forces
    Behind the creation
    Of Man.

    And from out of the Fires of Creation
    There emerged Water
    And Air
    And Land.

12. This time the Creative Spirits
    Would guide the creation of Man,
    And though they were too ephemeral
    For contact with matter,
    They created Astrals
    Within ethereal forms,
    Links between Spirit and Matter,
    Which fashioned Earth's Elements
    Into physical bodies
    Capable of hosting Spirit.

Once more the evolutionary process began,
And the Moon exerted her pull
On the creative waters of Earth.

Physical Man,
Born of Mother Earth,
With his lower subtle bodies
Fashioned by the Moon,
Would be a home
Fit for Spiritual Man,
Projected from the light of the Sun.

And to echo the division
And the coming together
Of Spirit and Body
Man would be divided
To come together
As male and female.

13. Pure, Divine Spirit
    Is devoid of the fiery passion
    That goes into creation
    And so, unable to create,
    The higher gods remained behind.

    But these newly-evolved lunar gods
    Had not progressed
    Beyond the influence
    Of Karmic Law
    And still possessed a creative passion;
    Each of the seven Moon gods
    Would govern one of Earth's seven continents
    And bestow his qualities
    On the Race that would be dominant
    Through the rise and fall
    Of each continent.

And as the physical Moon
Would govern the cycles
Of all Earth-bound Life,
So the Spirit of the Moon
Would guide the spiritual growth of Man.

*Man fell to an ancient Earth as the shadow of his boneless Creator,
without form or substance*

STANZA IV: THE CREATION OF THE FIRST RACES

14. This is the story,
    O Lanoo,
    Of the journey
    Of the Pilgrim-Soul
    Which travels
    Through the seven states of being;
    From spiritual
    And intellectual
    Unconsciousness,
    Through Matter and experience,
    To self-consciousness,
    Self-awareness
    And Enlightenment.

    Before Spiritual Man could exist
    There had to be
    The essence of Spiritual Man,
    Possessed by the Lunar Gods,
    Which they breathed out
    As Brahma had breathed out
    The Universe.

    With the involution
    Of Spirit
    Into Matter
    Spirit would descend
    Through ever-thickening layers
    From the pure and innocent
    To the gross;
    And from the gross,
    Spirit, now with experience,
    Would ascend
    Through the levels
    Of understanding
    To the pure and wise.

At the same time
Physical evolution developed
From the simple
To the complex,
And these two evolutionary cycles
Came together,
The nadir of one
In the zenith of the other.

15. The seven classes of gods
     Would create the Seven Races
     Of Man on Earth,
     With his four lower
     And three higher principles.

     The First Race
     Was not born of the gods,
     But by their will;
     Man fell to an ancient Earth
     As the shadow
     Of his boneless creator,
     Without form
     Or substance.

     And as this Race of shadows
     Gave way to beings of more substance
     So the guiding, creative Spirits
     Endowed each succeeding Race
     With the unique quality
     Inherent in each class of Creator.

     So it is that as Man evolves
     Each new Race is enhanced
     Until finally Man will come of age,
     With all his senses awakened,
     In the Seventh Race.

16. If early Man was without form
    How, then,
    O Lanoo,
    Was born
    The Man with Mind
    And Spirit
    And Body?

    The First Race of Man
    Emerged from the Astral essence
    Of those gods possessed
    With the creative fire.

    This Man was as insubstantial
    As a thought-form
    Created in your meditation;
    An empty phantom
    Without form or sense.

    Not until this Astral body
    Of the gods
    Merged with the Animal body
    Created by Nature
    Could Man stand
    And walk
    And fly.

    But this Second Race
    Still lacked the self-perception,
    The self-consciousness,
    That were to be the features
    Of Homo Sapiens;

Not until the gods
Who had held back
From the first stages of Creation
Fulfilled their destiny
By accepting rebirth
Was the Divine Spark in Man
Given expression.

Now, in Man,
There lived the three creative fires,
Of the Moon,
And of the Sun,
And of the Earth.

And whereas animals progressed unconsciously
Man could now look beyond his body
And recognise,
However dimly,
His ultimate goal:
To take his place,
Through his own efforts,
With the Gods.

17. These were the origins
Of septenary Man:
A physical body
With emotions
And Life Force
Clothed in an Astral body;
The four lower principles,
Supporting the three higher principles
Of Mind
And Soul
And Spirit.

This would be the miracle of Man:
The seven cosmic Elements
Brought together
On the seven planes of being
By the seven creative energies.

And though each Man
Possessed the essence
Of all seven principles,
In most men the principles would lie dormant
Until sparked by the creative energy
Of each new Age.

*The shadowy beings of the First Race were absorbed
into the more physical bodies of the Second Race*

STANZA V: THE EVOLUTION OF THE SECOND RACE

18. The gods created the First Race of Man
    From their own shadows,
    Or Astral bodies.

    But these were lesser Gods,
    The Creators of this First Race,
    For pure Spirit emerging
    From the long Night of Darkness
    Has no shadow
    And cannot create.

    The First Race
    Gave way to the Second Race
    As the life-giving Fire of the Sun
    And the motion in the waters
    Produced by the Moon
    Came together on Earth
    And Spirit entered the essence of Matter.

    But the essence of Man
    Was dormant,
    Awaiting the Spiritual Fire
    Which would through
    Sensory experience
    Bring together
    His Spirit, Soul and Mind
    In enlightened self-consciousness.

19. As Spirit fell deeper into Matter
    The formless shadows of the First Race
    Evolved, by a process akin
    To budding and expansion,
    Into the asexual beings
    Of the Second Race.

For just as the nucleus
Extrudes through the surface
Of the germ-cell,
O Lanoo,
So the Astral body
Extruded through the Auric sheath,
And nourished by the original cells,
The new Astrals grew and separated
Into the Second Race.

20. Thus did First Race Man,
    Self-born sons of the Gods,
    Become the fathers
    Of the Second Race.

    And in readiness
    For the separation of the sexes
    Which would come
    With more physical races,
    These Second Race beings
    Developed the rudimentary reproductive organs
    Of the hermaphrodite,
    Adopting a bisexual element
    Common to many of your ancient myths
    Of Gods and Mortals
    And still present,
    O Lanoo,
    In the bodies of your Fifth Race Man.

21. But this is a story of evolution
    And the Second Race did not suddenly appear.
    Gradually,
    Over aeons,
    The shadowy beings of the First Race
    Were absorbed
    Into the more physical bodies
    Of the Second Race,
    Not becoming extinct
    But living on in a new form.

The androgynous being of the Second Race gave way to the sexually separated male and female whose Age you now know, O Lanoo, as Lemuria

STANZA VI: THE SECOND RACE
GIVES WAY TO THE THIRD

22. The early Races of Man
Lived in their Garden of Eden,
Shadowy beings in an unearthly paradise,
Not subject to disease or physical decay,
Unaffected by the severe
Climactic and geological changes
That rocked the world.

But as Earth began to stabilise,
Slowly becoming a world
Capable of supporting physical life,
The descent of Spirit into Matter continued
And the Third Race appeared.

The Astral extrusions of the Second Race
Became more dense
And reproduction now took place
By the exudation of drops of moisture
Which coalesced,
Egg-like,
To be warmed by the Sun
And stirred by the Moon.

Throughout the period
Occupied by the Third Race,
Man became ever more physical,
And unable to exude offspring
Through his thickening skin
The androgynous being of the Second Race
Gave way to the sexually separated
Male and female
Whose Age you now know,
O Lanoo,
As Lemuria.

23. The Sons of the Gods
    Of the First Race,
    Being non-physical,
    Were immortal,
    But the Second Race
    Into which the First was absorbed
    Was subject to the laws of physics,
    And was decimated
    By the first
    Of Earth's great deluges.

    The story of the flood,
    O Lanoo,
    Is a confusion
    Of several stories
    Of several floods,
    With allegory and fact interwoven.

    The Atlantean Fourth Race
    Came to an end
    In a physical flood,
    But the story
    Also symbolises
    The salvation of Man
    At the end of the Third Race.

    Swamped by condensing matter,
    And unable to reproduce
    Except by the separation of the sexes,
    The seed of physical Man
    Was saved by the womb of Woman,
    Sailing like an ark
    Into the Fourth Race.

The Third Race moved towards sexual division
and the Fall of Man into the Fourth Race

STANZA VII: THE FIRST HUMAN RACES

24. Not all the lesser Gods
    Who guided the Creation
    Of the First Race of Man
    Incarnated in those early forms.

    One third of the Creative Spirits
    Entered the shadowy forms completely;
    Another third merely projected a spark;
    The final third chose to wait.

    Thus, whilst the physical evolution
    Of the beings who became Man
    Progressed deeper and deeper into Matter
    There were three distinct strands
    Of Spiritual evolution.

    There were those who developed an intellect
    And a karmic burden;
    They appeared worldly wise
    To those innocents
    Who did not enter the karmic stream
    Until much later;
    And there were those
    Who had a spiritual spark
    Yet lived in ignorance,
    Unable to achieve the union
    Of Spirit, Soul and Mind
    That was the birthright of Man.

25. But the Sons of Wisdom
    Chose not to enter
    The formless bodies
    Of the First Race,
    Born by the will of the Gods;

They chose not to enter
The Second Race,
Exuded like sweat
From the shadows of the Gods;
They chose not to enter
The egg-born bodies
Of the early Third Race.

Thus was established
The principle of free will,
Enjoyed by all men and women
Even as they fulfil their destiny.

The legends talk of Fallen Angels,
The ones who refused to create,
Who disobeyed God,
But whether the Fallen Angels
Would not incarnate
Or could not incarnate
Is not for you to decide,
O Lanoo.

Seek not to blame without understanding;
Look not for a force of evil
To counterbalance the force of good,
For all forces are aspects
Of the same God.

26. Not until the end
Of the Third Race,
When the body of Man hardened
And divided into male and female,
Did the Sons of Wisdom
Add their essence
To the beings
Who would be
The real Fathers of Man.

27. The First Race
    Were the shadows of their creators;
    Their "bodies" were devoid of understanding,
    Surrounded by the Divine Spirit
    But not yet connected.

    The Second Race,
    The sweat-born,
    Emanated from the shadows
    As if by budding,
    And contained the germ of intelligence.

    The egg-born
    Of the Third Race
    Was host to the Divine Spark,
    And Man now had
    Mind
    And body
    And spirit.

    And so by Thought alone
    Were created
    The spiritual forefathers
    Of the Masters
    Who would appear
    In the Fourth Race;
    For Creation is but the result
    Of Thought
    Or Will
    Acting on Matter.

    Thus were the Masters created
    By immaculate Thought
    As the Third Race
    Moved towards sexual division
    And the Fall of Man
    Into the Fourth Race.

*And that part of Mankind which had evolved without the Divine
Spark bred with animals and created a dumb race of creatures,
covered in hair and going on all fours*

STANZA VIII: THE ANIMAL KINGDOM
& THE FIRST FALL

28. Your Scriptures tell you,
    O Lanoo,
    That God created Earth
    And her vegetation
    And animals
    Before He created Man;
    This is the history
    Of the first three Races.

    And then
    In apparent contradiction
    The Scriptures tell that
    God formed Man of the dust of the ground
    And then out of the ground
    He formed every beast of the field;
    But this is the story
    Of the Fourth Race.

    And in this Fourth Round
    Man preceded the animals
    And all were formed
    Out of the physical elements
    Which were the debris
    Of those earlier Rounds.

29. And the animals evolved,
    Developing bones
    And limbs
    And wings;
    Dragons and serpents
    Living in the water
    And on the land
    And in the air.

30. During the Third Race of Man
    The animals also descended
    Into Matter,
    And as their bones developed
    Their bodies hardened
    Into the creatures that were
    The ancestors
    Of those animals you see today.

31. The animals,
    Now with solid bodies,
    Separated into male and female
    To reproduce,
    And Man watched them breed
    And did likewise.

32. And that part of Mankind
    Which had evolved
    Without the Divine Spark
    Bred with animals
    And created a dumb race
    Of creatures,
    Covered in hair
    And going on all fours.
    And although this might be thought of
    As the Fall of Man into sin
    No blame could attach to those beings
    Without the Divine Spark;
    The karmic burden
    Of this tragedy
    Fell upon those lesser Gods
    Who had as yet
    Chosen not to incarnate.

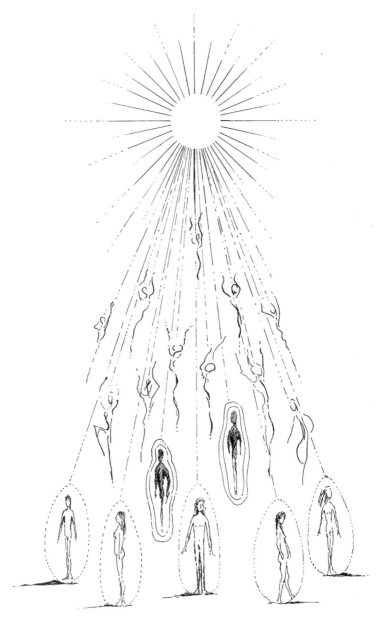

*The Rays appeared, to Man's clouded perception,
to be separate and discrete as they entered
the individual physical forms evolving on Earth*

STANZA IX: THE FINAL EVOLUTION
OF (PHYSICAL) MAN

33. The Spirits who had not incarnated,
    Who had refused to create,
    Looked down on this physical world
    And watched the soul-less men
    Breeding with animals.

    They saw the consequences of their inaction
    And wept.

34. They saw that the mindless beings
    Were defiling their own bodies
    And, accepting their Karma,
    They determined to incarnate,
    Lest Man degenerate completely.

    And so these Spirits appeared
    In the Fourth Race of Man,
    Living side by side
    With those Spirits
    Who had already experienced
    Many incarnations
    Through those earlier ages of Man.

    Thus, O Lanoo,
    Did your ancestors appear:
    Born into sin,
    Or rather, born with the sin
    Of having neglected those earlier beings.

35. This then was the Fourth Race:
    Dense physical bodies
    Separated into the sexes
    With Minds
    And Souls
    Illuminated by the Universal Ray
    Of the Divine Spirit;
    Souls which are forever aspiring
    To move beyond the confines of the body;
    Bodies which respond to the sensory stimuli
    Of this physical world;
    And minds
    Which are capable of understanding
    The benefits of experience
    And the burden of Karma.

    The first three Races of Man
    Descended from Spirit
    Into Matter.

    But in the Fourth Race
    The Fall of Man was complete;
    For in the next three Races
    Man will rise,
    Now possessing the wisdom
    Bought with experience,
    From Matter
    Into Spirit.

36. The Rays
    Emanating from The One
    Absolute Principle
    Fell on early Man,
    Mutating his physical evolution
    Into a form
    Which could accommodate
    The Divine Spirit.

Whilst remaining part
Of the Universal Essence
The Rays appeared,
To Man's clouded perception,
To be separate
And discrete
As they entered
The individual physical forms
Evolving on Earth.

And as Spirit
Moved into undeveloped minds
And bodies ever denser
So there grew in Man a sense of isolation.

The need for speech arose
And communication took the place of commu-
nion,
Simple grunts developed into complex language,
And Man,
In his ignorance,
Thought that words could bridge the gulf
Between individuals.

37. And as Man and the animals
    Separated into the sexes,
    And the boneless creatures
    Of the earlier races
    Became Fourth Race Man,
    The Man of the rib of Adam,
    The Creation of physical Man,
    Filled with the false pride
    Of his individuality,
    Was complete.

And when the Gods faded from his field of vision,
Man saw himself as King of Earth and believed he was a God

STANZA X: THE HISTORY OF THE FOURTH RACE

38. Thus two by two,
    Separated into the sexes,
    The Third Race gave birth
    To the Fourth Race,
    Which dwelt in the physical world,
    A world whose God became known
    As Satan,
    The Adversary.

    But Satan was a manifestation of God,
    Not an adversary,
    Rather it was Matter,
    The substance of Satan's world,
    That could be said to be opposed to Spirit.

    In each of the seven zones of earth
    The Sons of Gods
    Gave birth to physical Man,
    And for the first time
    The Divine Spark was
    Separated by a wall of Matter
    From the Divine Source.

    From some bodies
    The Divine Spark could dimly perceive
    The Divine Spirit,
    But most Men and Women
    Quickly forgot their divine nature.

39. The Gods
    The demi-Gods
    And the Heroes,
    The first three Races,
    Had little substance;
    But as Man became more dense
    So he could no longer create
    And with the fall of the Third Race
    Creation gave way to reproduction.

    This was the advent of the Fourth Race,
    The age of Atlantis,
    The world of the Titans;
    Man was human
    And terrestrial
    In every sense,
    With Mind
    And Nature
    Working together in Matter.

    The new, thickening skin
    Which clothed the subtle bodies
    Of the men who bridged
    The Third and Fourth Races
    Was uniform and moon-coloured,
    But in Fourth Race Man
    The pigmentation of this covering
    Would come to reflect
    The energies of the subtle bodies.

    The three distinct strands
    Of incarnating Souls,
    From the three different groups
    Of Creative Spirits,
    Established the three main sub-races of Atlantis.

The yellow,
The red,
And the brown
Would sub-divide
In the Seven Ages of the Fourth Race,
Producing the ancestors
Of the complex ethnic groups
In the Fifth Race of Man.

40. The separation of the sexes
Which began in the latter half
Of the Third Race
Was to evolve fully
In the Fourth Race;
The Age of Lemuria
Gave way to the Age of Atlantis.

As yet Man still communed with the Gods,
Not realising
That his slow fall into Matter
Rendered him less than the Gods.
And when the Gods
Faded from his field of vision
Man saw himself as King of Earth,
And believed that he was a God;
The ego eclipsed the Divine Spark
And Spiritual Man
Became the Man of Self.

41. The Golden Age
Became a distant memory,
For although the Gods
Were still with Man
Man could no longer perceive the Gods
And felt abandoned
In an Age of Darkness.

Now men responded to physical urges
And they took wives from each other,
And from lesser species;
Thus it was that
Ego battled with ego,
Man with Man,
And poor Earth knew
For the first time
The meaning of war.

42. Now, O Lanoo,
    Man could see no further
    Than his own body,
    Which thus became an object of worship,
    And his whole life
    Was dedicated to satisfying
    His basic desires.

    Man lost the ability to sense
    All but the lower vibrations
    Through his five lower senses;
    The third eye,
    The true window of the soul,
    Receded and atrophied
    Leaving the pineal gland
    As a sad reminder
    Of a distant glorious past
    When the art of "seeing"
    Embraced eternity.

    And with the loss of his third eye
    Man lost sight of the perfect harmony
    Of the Universe,
    Balanced by the law of Karma and Rebirth
    Which decrees that every action has a reaction;
    Every cause has an effect.

Man forgot that his Soul
Is subject to no Fate,
Random or predetermined,
Save that which every Being
Creates for himself.

And as his higher senses faded
Man became imprisoned
In a physical body
Constrained by Time and Space.

The destruction of Atlantis . . . by the deluge,
remembered in all your cultures

STANZA XI: THE DESTRUCTION OF THE FOURTH RACE

43. Thus the Third Race
    Was the first that you
    O Lanoo,
    Would recognise as Man;
    For though he dwelt with the Gods
    And would to you have seemed a giant
    Yet he was to become physical.

    During the seven sub-races
    Of those people you call Lemurians
    Their resonance,
    Their rate of vibration,
    Moved ever lower
    Until the needs of the body and the ego
    Dominated the Spirit.

    The sixth sub-race built huge cities
    From lava and marble,
    And from metals fashioned from the earth,
    And as the Age of Lemuria
    Neared its end
    So began the Age of Atlantis,
    The Fourth Race.

    There is no sudden end to an Age
    For the Races evolve
    One from the other,
    And so the people of a New Age
    Co-mingle with the people of the Old Age,
    Until finally the last traces of the old Race disap-
    pear.

And as the first Atlanteans began to appear
And the Lemurians lost contact with their gods
So the people used the lava
And the marble
To create giant, life-size statues
In their own image
Which in their ignorance they worshipped.

And the end of the Third Race came about
When Earth went through
Yet another convulsion.

She inclined her axis
And her crust groaned
And the volcanoes
And the raging seas
Broke up the continent of Lemuria,
In what would be remembered as
The twilight of the Gods on Earth.

And the cities
And the civilisations
Were destroyed,
With here and there
An island of survivors
With only memories
And myths
And fragments of relics
To share with their children.

44. Thus did the Fourth Race,
    The people of Atlantis,
    Emerge from the ruins of Lemuria,
    And again, seven sub-races
    In their turn
    Built cities and civilisations.

The final descent
From Spirit into Matter
Saw a decrease in Man's stature
As the early ethereal giants were compressed
Into the heavy bodies
Of the fourth sub-race
Of the Fourth Race.

Here, when Man was at the farthest point
From his spiritual ancestry and destiny
New "souls"
Ceased to incarnate.

Now would begin
The imperceptible movement
Up the cycle
As Man carried the wisdom of experience
Towards spirituality.
But as yet
The Atlanteans were no wiser
Than their ancestors;
Self was their only god
And again Man built statues
In his own likeness
To worship.

O Lanoo,
As Men of your own Fifth Race
Made their first appearance,
The destruction of Atlantis loomed;
Not, this time, by fire,
But by the deluge
Remembered in all your cultures.

45. The flood waters came
    And the continents of Atlantis
    Sank beneath the seas.

    This was no punishment
    Meted out to an ungodly people,
    But Evolution and Karma
    Working together;
    For just as each organism is born,
    Matures,
    Decays,
    And dies,
    So must each Life
    And each civilisation
    And each Race.

46. Once more,
    The people perished,
    And the animals,
    And now all those early,
    Mindless,
    Soul-less creatures,
    Had vanished for ever.

    But again there were survivors,
    On a scattering of islands,
    All that was left of mighty Atlantis;
    Small groups of men and women,
    And animals,
    Huddled together in misery,
    Became the link
    Between the Fourth Race
    And the Fifth Race.

Legend decrees
That through all the ages of Earth,
Through the fires
And volcanoes
And floods,
One piece of land shall survive intact.

At each time of destruction
A small number of Adepts
Gather in this sacred place
To ensure that the truth is remembered
And carried forward
From one Race to the next.

Myth and memory
Combine with ancient relics
To tantalise all generations
With what has gone before,
Yet the truth can be seen
By those with wisdom.

The ancient knowledge . . . would form the basis
of the belief systems of the Fifth Race

STANZA XII: THE FIFTH RACE

47. Your own chronicles,
    O Lanoo,
    Begin with the Fifth Race,
    But some memories
    Of earlier times
    Live on in myth
    And legend
    And religious teachings.

    Creation, Gods and angels;
    Floods and destruction;
    The Fall of Man;
    Fragments of real events
    From the first Four Races
    Are described and distorted
    As if all were the history
    Of your own Fifth Race.

    By now The First and Second Races
    And the early part of the Third Race
    Had gone forever,
    But there were some few remnants
    Of the different sub-races
    Of the Fourth Race
    Who survived the Atlantean flood.

    They brought with them
    Into the new age
    Some of the ancient knowledge,
    But Fifth Race Man
    Sensed they were different
    And they were persecuted and scorned.

48. As the Fourth Race neared its end
    Evolution produced a new strain of Man who,
    Descended from the Gods of earlier Races,
    Survived the Atlantean deluge
    In greater numbers than the old stock;
    And, ruled by kings with divine knowledge,
    These people became the dominant
    Fifth Race of today.

49. The Adepts who survived
    Dwelt in subterranean chambers
    Under mountains
    And ancient pyramids;
    They wrote down their history
    On tablets of stone
    And emerged
    To teach and instruct
    The Fifth Race.

    The ancient knowledge
    Was given to the new Race
    But sparingly,
    Often by parable,
    For after the deluge
    Life was very primitive;
    And these teachings
    And ancient writings,
    Often imperfectly interpreted,
    Would form the basis
    Of the belief systems
    Of the Fifth Race.

    And so,
    O Lanoo,
    You now know your own story,
    For the rest is well documented.

One day your people
Will be joined
By the forerunners of the Sixth Race,
And Man will leave behind
His temporary world of Matter
And move ever closer
To the spiritual destiny
That awaits the Seventh Race.

EPILOGUE

Behold, O Lanoo!
You are a seven-aspected Being,
A collection of atoms
And molecules
And subtle energies
Which are constantly changing,
Evolving,
Becoming,
In a Universe
Which is constantly changing,
Evolving,
Becoming.

You have become today
That which you were becoming yesterday,
So cling not
To that which was
But look at what is to be,
At what you are becoming,
For to resist this forward motion
Is to resist the very nature of the Universe.

And as you move towards
A spiritual destiny
Glorious beyond your imagination
Know that we are all Pilgrim-Souls
At different stages
Of the same journey.

And be not deluded into saying
"Thy Soul" and "my Soul"
For at the end of the journey
We will be as one.

The path is long
But be not overawed,
Nor feel insignificant or alone,
For whatever stage you have reached,
Like all Pilgrim-Souls,
You can do no more
Than take the next step.

And with every step
Know that you are truly sacred,
And that all sentient Beings are your kin,
For you are part of God
And God is all of you.